All scriptural references are taken from the
NIV, NASB and KJV
of the Holy Bible

ISBN: 978-9988-2-3341-9
© 2016

Author: Charles Nana Kwadwo Twumasi-Ankrah
kingdomtakeoverconferencesandsummits@gmail.com
prophnana1@gmail.com
(+233) 0243 959 511

Published and Printed by
Paper & Ink Media
(+233) 0277 439 086

Cover Design & Layout by
Daniford Images
(+233) 057 311 3653

Written permission must be secured from the publisher
to use or reproduce any part of this book, except for
brief quotations in critical reviews or articles

CONTENTS

Dedication	p4
About the Author	p5
Forward	p7
Acknowledgement	p8
Introduction	p9
Chapter One (SENSE OF VALUES)	p13
Chapter Two (VIRTUES)	p61
EPILOGUE	p92

DEDICATION

I have the singular honour to dedicate this book to VERITY DODOO. You have added colour to my personality and ministry as well. I love you dear one!

ABOUT THE AUTHOR

Charles Nana Kwadwo Twumasi-Ankrah is a servant in the vineyard of God. Charles is a preacher and teacher of the word. He ministers at crusades and conferences both locally and internationally.

Charles is dedicated to the things of God. His uttermost passion is to see the revival of the move of God across the globe with the motive of preparing the Body of Christ for the return of the Lord Jesus Christ.

He is a revivalist with an uncompromising message on discipleship, kingdom pursuits, purpose, faith, love, righteousness, divine manifestations, as well as unearthing

FOREWORD BY
VERY REV. GEORGE WESLEY TAGOE

Values & Virtues

CHARLES NANA K. TWUMASI-ANKRAH

Values & Virtues

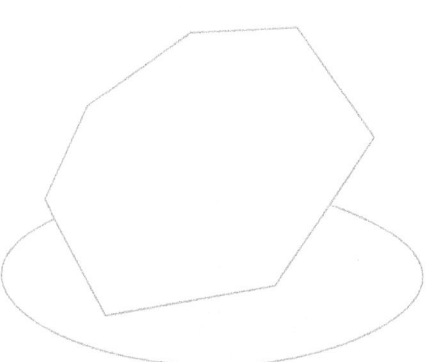

potentials and capabilities.

Charles is the founder of Kingdom Take Over Conferences and Summits (KTOCS); a Christian based conference destined to train, equip and shape lives.

B.A (POL. STDS, KNUST), M.A (MINISTRY, TRINITY THEOLOGICAL SEMINARY)

FOREWORD

This is a masterpiece from the author of "The Revival –A voice in the End Time", "Divine Mandate" and "Value Series".

"The LORD does not see as man sees. For man looks at the outward appearance, but God looks at the heart.

In the midst of His brothers; David was anointed and the Spirit of the LORD came upon him" I Sam 16:7, 13. By human standards, the selection process should have started with the older brothers, but he chose the youngest.

I remember the days of simple beginning when the author will just pick his android phone, write a verse of scripture, expand it and forward it to all contacts on his phone and to facebook as well. Little by little the "Value Series" that we all yearn to read daily has ended up in this beautiful and educative piece.

We do not have to despise simple beginning since we do not know where it will end. The God who sees the end from the beginning will add his blessings for this book to have its full impact on all who will read it.

Verity Dodoo

ACKNOWLEDGEMENT

I thank God for His divine wisdom and guidance in leading me to champion this cause. I am blessed to be used by God for His work. I say thank you my Lord and King for counting on me as a vessel of honour, meet to be used in these end times.

To Ernestina Okoe-Martey, you have done a very good job. Thank you for devoting yourself to editing this series daily. Now it's a masterpiece and the credit goes to you. As people get impacted, so your blessing will be.

Many thanks goes to Mr Yaw Asiedu-Danquah and Dr Esinam Ata Akunnor for their timely words of knowledge that have helped shaped this material. May you increase abundantly on every side.

Mr Daniel Boakye Denteh, I cannot thank you enough. You have played a key role in moulding me and for the success I have made in life and ministry, you have been instrumental. The exceptional designs you always give to my books and posters are really appreciated. May God bless you in His own marvelous ways.

To my wide-read audience, thank you for your feedbacks and co-operation. This is what we have all been waiting for and today, it is here with us. It is now a manual to all of us. You all made it happen and I am very grateful.

Be blessed by it!

INTRODUCTION

Life must be cherished and given full attention. The essence of life is for one to make it worth living. It is good and awesome when you make life simple for yourself and for others.

Your life is yours and it is in your hands. Although God sees to the affairs of men, your life is never His until you entrust your life into His hands. You live for yourself, family, society and country at large and most importantly for God. A life without Christ is crisis in disguise. In the same vein, a life without values and virtues is misery.

Life is full of ethics, that need to be applied on a daily basis. To be ethically bankrupt means living no meaningful and impactful life. A good life is rich with morals, resulting in good standards of living. A life well lived, overflows with values and virtues.

There are four types of personal value systems, namely: personal values, spiritual values, family values and career values.

Personal values are those traits we see as worth aspiring for and they define our character. When our personality is refined, we become assets to many people.

Spiritual Values are values that connect us to a higher power and give us a sense of purpose beyond our material existence. When we are spiritually inclined, walking in truth, purity and righteousness will not be difficult for us. Our spiritual senses do shape us and connect us much to God.

Family values lead us to love and care for those we are close to: our children, parents, spouses, siblings, other relatives and our friends.
Career Values is the best use and expressions of our talents and skills for the purposes of contributing to society and for monetary compensation.

No matter what tradition we are brought up in, there are characteristics we value in others which transcend social, economic and religious boundaries.

Some of these characteristics are:
1. Integrity - trustworthiness, honesty and uprightness of character. We value people of integrity because we know what to expect from

them. We know they will act honorably and do what they think is right. We want people with integrity as our friends, on our teams and in our organizations. Therefore when we keep our integrity in good shape, we will attract men of such class.

2. *Respect* - honoring the worth and dignity of all people. Those who respect others treat them with fairness and courtesy. They treat others the way they would like to be treated themselves. Do not forget that, whatever you respect, you will attract!

3. *Loyalty* - commitment and faithfulness to a person or cause. Those who are loyal to their families, friends, organizations, countries and their God, stand behind and support them during good times and bad times. They can be counted on to be there when the going gets difficult and to help out when the chips are down. Loyalty is a great virtue to ride on to success. When you are loyal, many people will count on you.

4. *Responsibility* - those who accept responsibility are reliable, dependable and willing to take accountability for who they are and what they do. They believe they have a moral obligation to help others and make a contribution to the society they live in.

Knowing the values you want to live by, it is vital that you look at the bigger picture, assess what you want your role to be, and map out how you intend to conduct your life. Do bear in mind that, the values that control your thoughts and behavior, shapes what you value or what you are ready to die for. For example, a person who does not have a personal value of truth cannot value God. There is always a connection between our personal values and what we are ready to follow, sacrifice for or defend.

VALUE One

HAVING THE SENSE OF
VALUE

*O**n the third day there was a wedding in Cana of Galilee, and the mother of Jesus was there; and both Jesus and His disciples were invited to the wedding. When the wine ran out, the mother of Jesus said to Him, "They have no wine." And Jesus said to her, "Woman, what does that have to with us? My hour has not yet come." His mother said to the servants, "Whatever He says to you, do it." Now* *there were six stone waterpots set there for the Jewish custom of purification, containing twenty or thirty gallons each. Jesus said to them, "Fill the waterpots with water." So they filled them up to the brim. And e said to them, "Draw some out now and take it to the headwaiter." So they took it to him. When the headwaiter tasted the water which had become wine, and did not know where it came from (but the servants who had drawn the water knew), the headwaiter called the bridegroom, and said to him, "Every man serves the good wine first, and when the people have drunk freely, then he serves the poorer wine; but you have kept the good wine until now."*

John 2:1-10

Value is a powerful tool in life. What you place value on determines the kind of results you get in the end

To value means to cherish, hold in high esteem, place priority and essence on something.

Jonathan valued the relationship he had with David therefore his descendants became blessed.

Mary placed value on Jesus' grace & anointing. By so doing, Jesus performed that miracle in Canaan. Mary valued the words of her son Jesus and cautioned the people to obey whatever instructions he gave them. The importance of value in the realm of personality made the people have wine in excess.

You cannot withdraw from the bank if you have no money in your bank account. It is your level of deposit that will determine your level of withdrawal. If you place value on what you carry, you will definitely excel.

VALUE Two

HAVING THE SENSE OF VALUE
LIVING IN WISDOM

By wisdom a house is built, And by understanding it is established; And by knowledge the rooms are filled with all precious and pleasant riches. A wise man is strong, And a man of knowledge increases power. For by wise guidance you will wage war, And in abundance of counselors there is victory. Wisdom is too exalted for a fool, He does not open his mouth in the gate.

Proverbs 24: 3-7

It is important for every believer to live in wisdom. Life will be of no meaning if there is inability to think or act using knowledge, experience, understanding, common sense and insight.

Many people are not as knowledgeable as they may look . Whiles others seek daily for insights and fight not to live in ignorance, others desire much to dwell in foolishness.

In our world today, we have educated men and women whose reasoning patterns have been taken by the lust of this world, their affluence, politics and even by the manipulations of men.

The wisest man who ever lived said: "teach us to number our days that we can apply our hearts with wisdom". In this regard, life demands daily personal evaluations, to build up on experiences and utilize the insight we gain for the journey ahead.

Let your heart be quick to acquire wisdom and your ear fast to seek knowledge. Think over what I say, for the Lord will give you understanding in everything.

You hardly ask God to increase you in wisdom. This is an opportunity to ask the Lord for wisdom, knowledge, understanding and insight (Pray)

> *Therefore be careful how you walk, not as unwise men but as wise, making the most of your time, because the days are evil. So then do not be foolish, but understand what the will of the Lord is.*
> *Ephesians 5: 15-17*

VALUE Three

HAVING THE SENSE OF VALUE
YOUR SALVATION

He entered into Jericho and was passing through. And there was a man called by the name Zaccheus; he was a chief tax collector and he was rich. Zaccheus was trying to see who Jesus was, and was unable because of the crowd, for he was small in stature. So he ran on ahead and climbed up into a sycamore tree in order to see Him, for he was about to pass through that way. When Jesus came to the place, He looked up and said to him, "Zaccheus, hurry and come down, for today I must stay at your house." And he hurried and came down and received Him gladly. When they saw it they all began to grumble, saying," He has gone to be the guest of a man who is a sinner." Zaccheus stopped and said to the Lord, "Behold, Lord, half of my possessions I will give to the poor, and if I have defrauded anyone of anything, I will give back four times as much." And Jesus said to him, "Today salvation has come to this house, because he, too, is a son of Abraham. "For the Son if Man has come to seek and save that which was lost."

Luke 19: 1-10

Life presents a lot of things that need to be valued. The greatest of these is Salvation. In the realm of sin, God saved the world through His only Son, Jesus Christ. Life without salvation is vague.

Salvation means to be brought out, redeemed, released and saved from sin or bondage into freedom.

Zacchaeus was a rich man but lacked salvation. His reaction to catch a glimpse of Jesus showed how he yearned to be saved. He valued money but at the hour of salvation, money was a vexation of spirit and vanity to him

When you value something, you go all out for it. Salvation is not a one day deal, but an everyday process unto eternity.

For salvation ye have not just received but by the grace of God. You are not to ask for salvation. Rather, work it out daily with fear and

VALUE Four

HAVING THE SENSE OF VALUE
LIFE, OH LIFE!

Wisdom along with an inheritance is good and an advantage to those who see the sun. For wisdom is protection just as money is protection, but the advantage of knowledge is that wisdom preserves the lives of its possessors.

Ecclesiastes 7: 11-12

Life is precious and should be valued as such.

Many people do take certain life events for granted. It is prudent to have a sense of value, because without that, there will be no fruitfulness.

That is why there is the need to evaluate your life at any point in time to know whether you are on the right path or not. This helps one to assess himself and adjust.

The wisest man who ever lived said: "teach us to number our days that we can apply our hearts unto wisdom". We need to know the limited time we have to spend here on earth, lest we drift away from the Lord and not see the value of our lives.

Cooperation, commitment, focus, zeal, faithfulness and devotion are virtues we cannot live without. I have heard a lot of people say: "my life is in the hands of God", whiles they sit and fold their arms expecting manna to fall from heaven.

Go through the academic cycle with the aim of studying to show yourself approved. Work diligently and the promotion will come in due course. Do not bang everything on God; for it is man's duty to work and that of God's to bless

The value you place on your life determines who you become. If you spend your time chasing after women, drinking or smoking, the result is obvious. Value your life from today and see yourself flourish.

> *So teach us to number our days, That we may present to You a heart of wisdom.*
> *Psalm 90:12*

VALUE Five

HAVING THE SENSE OF VALUE
YOUR INTEGRITY MY INTEGRITY

> *Finally, brethren, whatever is true, whatever is honorable, whatever is right, whatever is pure, whatever is lovely, whatever is of good repute, if there is any excellence and if anything worthy of praise, dwell on these things.*
>
> *Philippians 4:8*

Integrity is trustworthiness, honesty and uprightness of character. We value people of integrity because we know what to expect from them. We know they will act honorably and that they will do what they think is right. We want people with integrity as our friends, on our teams and in our organizations.

We are not to be honorable only in the Lord's sight but also in the sight of men. Whoever walks in integrity walks securely but he who makes his ways crooked will be found out.

Be faithful in the Lord's house. At the work place be upright. In the community, let your honesty be known by all and in the family, let your deeds be pure and just.

> *He who walks in integrity walks securely, but he who perverts his ways will be found out.*
> *Proverbs 10:9*

VALUE YOUR INTEGRITY!

VALUE Six

HAVING THE SENSE OF VALUE
FORGIVENESS

I appeal to you for my child Onesimus, whom I have begotten in my imprisonment, who formerly was useless to you, but now is useful both to you and to me. I have sent him back to you in person, that is, sending my very heart, whom I wished to keep with me, so that on your behalf he might minister to me in my imprisonment for the gospel; but without your consent I did not want to do anything, so that your goodness would not be, in

> *effect, by compulsion but of your own free will. For perhaps he was for this reason separated from you for a while, that you would have him back forever, no longer as a slave, but more than a slave, a beloved brother, specially to me, but how much more to you, both in the flesh and in the Lord. If then you regard me a partner, accept him as you would me. But if he has wronged you in any way or owes you anything, charge that to my account; I, Paul, am writing this with my own hand, I will repay it (not to mention to you that you owe to me even your own self as well). Yes, brother, let me benefit from you in the Lord; refresh my heart in Christ.*
>
> *Philemon 1: 10-20*

Today, I touch on the subject of FORGIVENESS.

Many relationships and family ties have been broken due to unforgiveness. It is sad to know how fruitful and great unions have been disrupted due to the spirit of unforgiveness.

In as much as it is not easy to forgive, we need to recognize the fact that unforgiveness holds back many blessings from us. Whenever you place value on relationships, forgiveness must be a tool to sustaining a good and lasting one especially in times of disunity.

When our numerous sins rendered us naked, God forgave us and offered His only son, Jesus Christ, as a ransom to purge us from our sinful nature.

God blotted out the sins of our forefathers and their iniquities, He remembered no more. The story is not different with our generation.

Maybe your parents did not cater for you but today by the grace of God you have made it in life; do forgive and honor them as scripture says. You may have been offended by a close relative some time back, do forgive them and do not let bitterness take you away from God's blessings.

The man forgave his prodigal son after wasting all those resources. Paul admonished Philemon to take back Onesimus based on forgiveness.
I have heard lots of people say: "as for this wrong you have done to me, I have forgiven you but I cannot forget".

Can you imagine God keeping daily records of your sins even after you have admitted your faults and asked for pardon?

God's mind is not like the computer which has a recycle bin and with an option to restore all deleted items. When God grants you pardon of a fault committed, you are forgiven indeed. The joy of this is that your sins are not remembered anymore.

When people wrong you, forgive them and do not keep the wrong deeds in your records. Empty your records full of people's misdeeds because even your sins that you acknowledge have been washed away and are not in God's file.

> *I, even I am the one who wipe out your transgressions for my own sake, And I will not remember your sins. "Put Me in remembrance, let us argue our case together; State your cause, that you may be proved right.*

Isaiah 43: 25-26

WHEN YOU FORGIVE, DO FORGET ABOUT IT...LOOSE SOMEONE NOW!

LET GO AND LET GOD!

VALUE Seven

HAVING THE SENSE OF VALUE
LIVING RIGHT

Do this, knowing the time, that it is already the hour for you to awaken from sleep; for now salvation is nearer to us than when we believed. The night is almost gone, and the day is near. Therefore let us lay aside the deeds of darkness and put on the armor of light. Let us behave properly as in the day, not in carousing and drunkenness, not in sexual promiscuity and sensuality, not in strife and jealousy. But put on the Lord Jesus Christ,

> *and make no provision for the flesh in regard to its lusts.*
>
> *Romans 13:11-14*

We need to live right always, irrespective of where we find ourselves. Living right is the best contribution you can make to your life.

Life is precious and should not be lived anyhow. Every worthy cause in life must be approached in the right way, for impact to be made.

Many people have a problem understanding the word: 'RIGTHEOUSNESS'. The word in its simplest form means: 'to LIVE RIGHT'.

PREAMBLES: How difficult is it to stand for what is right? Is it that difficult to stay away without gossiping about someone? How difficult is it to write the exact time you reported at work (when you know very well that you reported late)? Must you tell a lie to survive whiles you know the truth? Etc.

In the light of these, a conscious effort should be made to live right, so that we attain a state of wholeness.

LIVING RIGHT: A GUIDE TO PERFECTION!
> *Do not be deceived, God is not mocked; for whatever a man sows, this he will also reap. For the one who sows to his own flesh will from the flesh reap corruption, but the one who sows to the*

> *Spirit will from the Spirit reap eternal life.*
> *Galatians 6: 7-8*

Whenever you live right, you become an envy to many who do not live same. This means that a level of righteousness is enviable.

In a community, where dubious means is the order of the day of doing things; to live right in such environment will erode the standard of evil. It is interesting to say that the brothers of Joseph plotted to kill him but it took Reuben to stand and say 'to kill him is to the extreme but let us spare his life'. Though the exercise carried out in the end was not right; Reuben's suggestion brought a sense of what must be done right.

In the mist of unrighteousness, living right is difficult. It is not easy to always carry out strong values of living right. To live right opens one to criticisms, mockery and ridicule. When you stand for truth the masses who sing a different chorus will not like you.

It is worth noting that a little light of your honesty, trustworthiness, truthfulness, faithfulness and a lifestyle of being just will triumph over evil deeds exhibited anywhere you find yourself. Remember, if darkness could not comprehend what the light gave in the beginning of creation; this same light will penetrate through any evil.

LIVING RIGHT: A LIGHT ON OUR PATH!!!

VALUE Eight

HAVING THE SENSE OF VALUE
STUDY

"You shall therefore impress these words of mine on your heart and on your soul; and you shall bind them as a sign on your hand, and they shall be as frontals on your forehead. "You shall teach them to your sons, talking of them when you sit in your house and when you walk along the road and when you lie down and when you rise up. "You shall write them on the doorposts of your house and on your gates, so that your days and the days of your sons may be multiplied on the land which the

LORD swore to your fathers to give them, as long as the heavens remain above the earth. "For if you are careful to keep all this commandment which I am commanding you to do, to love the LORD your God, to walk in all His ways and hold fast to Him, then the LORD will drive out all these nations from before you, and you will dispossess nations greater and mightier than you.
Deuteronomy 11:18-23

It is very necessary to avail yourself to study. Study forms part of life's foundation for success.

You need to study your books as you ought, read and study your bible daily. Develop an attitude of studying the character of people. Study enables you to uncover that which is covered.

Study is a guide of knowing the unknown. It breeds insight and makes you armed with information. The more you study, the more instrumental you become. A deeper level of study produces much wisdom.

Build your life on both informal and formal study. Study at home for insight into home ethics and desire to seek formal education in any form. Cultivate the attitude of reading books from various authors. This will help shape your mental ability.

Failure to study throws you into a state of ignorance. Seek always to be informed than to exhibit your ignorance at sensitive places. This can cost you fortunes that you may not be able to recover in life. When you are abreast with issues and you have mastery in a particular field, your delivery is excellent and your confidence will be up always. This tells you that whenever you are in the know you will certainly be in the flow.

> *Be diligent to present yourself approved to God as a workman who does not need to be ashamed, accurately handling the word of truth.*
>
> *2 Timothy 2:15*

STUDY: SUCCESS FOUNDATION

VALUE Nine

HAVING THE SENSE OF VALUE
MEDITATION

"Until I come, devote yourself to the public reading of Scripture, to preaching and to teaching. Do not neglect your gift, which was given you through prophecy when the body of elders laid their hands on you. Be diligent in these matters; give yourself wholly to them, so that everyone may see your progress".

1 Timothy 4:13-15

The ministry of the Holy Spirit leads me to touch on the subject of

'Meditation'. It is quite interesting to know that this subject is not valued by most people.

Meditation is a means of transforming the human mind. It is a level of awareness in the sense that whatever you think of in awareness is meditation. For example: becoming conscious of one's breath, is meditation. Meditation is a concentrated mental attention. It is a level of training given to the human mind.

One of the cheapest ways to digest things on earth, especially concerning scripture, is by means of meditation. Spiritually, when you give more attention to any scripture, you gain more insight and revelation into it. That is why at some points in the Bible, the word 'Selah' is used to end the passage or sentence; meaning 'its time to pause and consider or reflect on what you have read'. In doing so, you are thrown into a state of meditation.

In Daniel 12:1-4, it is noted that after Daniel studied and closed the books, knowledge continued to abound. How? Based on Daniel's careful reflections on what he read, knowledge increased in him. Reading the Bible without getting any insight or revelation can be equated to reading the dailies or a magazine.

Do not sit behind your books without any sense of meditation; that will not yield any good grades. Meditate on whatever you read and train your mind to digest what is read. Remember: what you read is not profitable until it is digested, just like what you eat is not useful until it undergoes the process of digestion.

MEDITATION: THE MIND TRAINER!

VALUE Ten

HAVING THE SENSE OF VALUE
PERSONAL EVALUATION

> *Now therefore, thus says the LORD of hosts, "Consider your ways!" "You have sown much, but harvest little; you eat, but there is not enough to be satisfied; you drink, but there is not enough to become drunk; you put on clothing, but no one is warm enough; and he who earns, earns wages to put into a purse with holes." Thus says the LORD of hosts, "Consider your ways!*
>
> Haggai 1:5-7

Having a sense of evaluation makes one concrete with facts, insight and helps build strong projections. Evaluation in itself brings a sense of value. Without personal evaluations, we make mistakes and mostly live in ignorance.

Many people lack personal evaluation, hence they accept any information, word or issue as it is. A lack of personal evaluation leads to manipulations and encroachment of reasoning and will.

One of the greatest personal evaluations we mostly lack happens when God takes us to a new environment, place or country. It is sad to point out that we rather prefer being seen at these new places to making evaluations concerning that particular place. Whenever God takes you to a new place, there is the need to know why He took you there (evaluation). Jesus had to go through Samaria and He needed to know what pertained to the land. In the end, the woman at Sychar was saved and that made His evaluation successful.

God has an eye on earthly relationships, be it friendship, marriage or family ties. Do we even evaluate our relationships? Out of our personal evaluations in relationships, we get a sense of purpose, bonding, trust, covenant and a tenacity to bond strongly always.

Living without a sense of personal evaluation at any point in time of your life is not healthy. As you live daily, take stock of your life.

> *Let us examine and probe our ways, And let us return to the LORD. Lamentations 3:40*

PERSONAL EVALUATION: A TOOL OF INSIGHT!

VALUE Eleven

HAVING THE SENSE OF VALUE
THE POWER OF DECISIONS

In Gibeon the LORD appeared to Solomon in a dream at night; and God said, "Ask what you wish me to give you." Then Solomon said, "You have shown great lovingkindness to Your servant David my father, according as he walked before You in truth and righteousness and uprightness of heart toward You; and You have reserved for him this great lovingkindness, that You have him a son to sit on his throne, as it is this day. " Now, O LORD

> *my God, You have made Your servant king in place of my father David, yet I am but a little child; I do not know how to go out or come in. "Your servant is in the midst of Your people which You have chosen, a great people who are too many to be numbered or counted. "So give Your servant an understanding heart to judge Your people to discern between good and evil. For who is able to judge this great people of Yours?" It was pleasing in the sight of the Lord that Solomon had asked this thing. God said to him, "Because you have asked this thing and have not asked for yourself long life, nor have asked riches for yourself, nor have you asked for the life of your enemies, but have asked for yourself discernment to understand justice, behold, I have done according to your words. Behold, I have given you a wise and discerning heart, so that there has been no one like you before God, nor shall one like you arise after you.*
>
> *1 Kings 3:5-12*

At every level of your personal evaluation, you must take a stance. There will be no essence in evaluation, if it is not complemented with a decision.

Many people re-examine their lives occasionally, but fail to change the wrong things due to lack of decision-making. That is why at the beginning of every year, a lot of people sit to make resolutions for the

New Year, yet fail to follow their own re-adjustments because of the lack of decisions.

Decisions bring out the clearer picture of your dreams and visions. When you decide on what to do or go for in life, you gain strength in that regard. Life without decision breeds misery.

The three wisemen had a task at hand, but based on their evaluation at the view of the star, they resolved to follow it and through that, they saw the Messiah and worshiped Him.

Matthew could not help but review himself to follow Jesus (decision). Peter dropped his net after evaluating his status in the fishing industry to follow Jesus (decision).

Today, re-examine yourself and see if there are any flaws or weaknesses. Even things that look good in your life can be relooked at for perfection.

DECISION: THE LIFE BUILDER!

VALUE Twelve

HAVING THE SENSE OF VALUE
PLANNING

By wisdom a house is built and by understanding it is established; And by knowledge the rooms are filled with all precious and pleasant riches.
Proverbs 24:3-4

It is needful to set up a pathways and channels suitable for achieving success. However, these should all run on the wheels of planning.

Planning is the eye for a successful change. If goals can be achieved, it is moulded on planning. You cannot go through life with open goals, ideas, visions and dreams without planning to manifest in these dimensions.

Having known your purpose, the next is to plan how to accomplish it. Planning is basically about thinking through or pondering over how to realize your set goals. Thinking is the principal tool for planning. In this regard, you need to think through before you labour. Do not go about sweating in life for nothing. Sit and map out a plan for your life.

It will take planning for every purpose to be accomplished and this can strongly be effected through the use of common sense. Don't just sit on the fence and fold your arms without doing anything. Put thoughts together and start to build your life. Desire not to be a talker by speaking on every issue. Rather, be a thinker and become a successful person.

Wisdom plays a vital role in the act of planning. Never forsake wisdom when planning because it takes wisdom to enable you locate the important things of your mission and what needs attention. This helps to put things together.

When you plan your life, you will not fail but when you fail to plan, the result is obvious.

Wisdom has built her house, She has hewn out her seven pillars
Proverbs 9:1

PLANNING: THE ROAD MAP TO YOUR DESTINATION!

VALUE Thirteen

HAVING THE SENSE OF VALUE
CHOICES

As he was going along by the Sea of Galilee, He saw Simon and Andrew, the brother of Simon, casting a net in the sea; for they were fishermen. And Jesus said to them, "Follow Me, and I will make you become fishers of men." Immediately they left their nets and followed Him. Going on a little farther, He saw James the son of Zebedee, and John his brother, who were also in the boat mending the nets. Immediately He called them;

> *and they left their father Zebedee in the boat with the hired servants, and went away to follow Him.*
> *Mark 1:16-20*

What actually influences a person's sense of value is the power to choose. Whiles others cherish personal values over spiritual values, others also give a strong endorsement to career values over family values.

No matter what values we choose to live by, it is vital that we look at the bigger picture, assess what we want our role to be, and map out how we intend to conduct our lives.

You see, the values that control your thoughts and behavior shapes what values or what you are ready to die for. For example a person who does not have a personal value of truth cannot value God. There is always a link between our personal values and what we are ready to follow, sacrifice for or defend.

At Galilee, they left their nets and chose Jesus because of value. Choose this day whom you will serve. As for me and my household, we will serve the Lord.

> *"If it is disagreeable in your sight to serve the LORD, choose for yourselves today whom you will serve: whether the gods which your fathers served which were beyond the River, or the gods of the*

Amorites in whose land are living; but as for me and my house, we will serve the LORD."
Joshua 24:15

VALUE Fourteen

HAVING THE SENSE OF VALUE
BE SENSITIVE ENOUGH

> *"Having lost all sensitivity, they have given themselves over to sensuality so as to indulge in every kind of impurity, and they are full of greed".*
> *Ephesians 4:19*

Life demands a level of sensitivity. We live in a physical world which is full of spiritual activities. Living life without any level of sensitivity is carnality.

Living a life to the dictates of the flesh will lead you to gratify the things of the flesh. Your level of sensitivity is a guide unto which path to walk on. The disciples of Jesus desired to know the particular time and season in which the Kingdom of God shall be restored to them but Jesus said: "it is not for you to know the times and season". We do not need to know what triggers the exact happenings or occurrences in our daily lives. The most important thing is to be sensitive enough.

Peter and his co-workers did not know that the fishes in the sea will be absent at the time of fishing. If they had any knowledge of that they would have rested on that day. Peter was sensitive at Jesus' saying and they caught a boat-full of fishes. The widow of Zarephath was sensitive at the word of the prophet and she had abundance to feed on in her home.

Zacchaeus was sensitive enough to tap into the salvation knowledge of God based on his level of expectancy and need.

Are you sensitive to words thrown at you daily? Do you pay heed to inscriptions on public transports, billboards, etc.? Are you lead by the Holy Spirit? Life is physical but it is the spiritual that feeds the physical. Do not live any how but be sensitive enough to the details of life patterns.

> *"and that they will come to their senses and escape from the trap of the devil, who has taken captive to do his will."*
> *2 Timothy 2:26*

LACK OF SENSITIVITY BREEDS SENSUALITY AND CALLOUSNESS

VALUE Fifteen

HAVING THE SENSE OF VALUE
WHEN IT IS YOUR TIME

> *"When Isaac was old and his eyes were so weak that he could no longer see, he called for Esau his older son and said to him, 'My son". "Here I am," he answered. Isaac said, "I am now an old man and don't know the day of death. Now then, get your equipment-your quiver and bow-and go out to open country to hunt some wild game for me. Prepare me the kind of tasty food I like and bring it to me to eat, so that I may give my blessing before I die." Now Rebekah was listening as Isaac spoke to his son Esau. When Esau left for the open*

> *country to hunt the game and bring it back, Rebekah said to her son Jacob, "Look, I overhead your father say to your brother Esau, 'Bring me some game and prepare me some tasty food to eat, so that I may give you my blessing in the presence of the LORD before I die.' Now, my son, listen carefully and do what I tell you: Go out to the flock and bring me two choice young goats, so I can prepare some tasty food for your father, just the way he likes it. Then take it to your father to eat, so that he may give you his blessing before he dies." Jacob said to Rebekah his mother, "But my brother Esau is a hairy man while I have smooth skin. What if my father touches me? I would appear to be tricking him and would bring down a curse on myself rather than a blessing." His mother said to him, "My son, let the curse fall on me. Just do what I say; go and get them for me."*
>
> *Genesis 27:1-13*

Everybody has just a day to manifest whatever God has said from eternity into time. All that you are looking for is subject to time. Anybody who is determined in life, constantly declares: "one day, I will make it".

The people of God were in captivity for long but when it was time for their deliverance, God showed up. Ziba referred to Mephibosheth as a leper and he emphasized on his weakness but when it was time, the limitation of Mephibosheth was overlooked.

It is worth noting that when it is your time, not everybody is on your side. Rebekah never rejoiced for Esau when his time of blessing came. Instead, she conspired with Jacob and made sure he was not blessed. The fact that you are getting married does not mean everybody is on your side. You are the least in your family and by the grace of God, you have made it - never think that everybody is on your side.

When it is your time, never be complacent. Esau knew that by order of birthright surely his father will give him the blessing before he departs. He was confident and banged all his hopes on that glorious day for his blessings but Jacob worked for it. Never be complacent whiles your miracle is not yet in your hands.

When it is your time, do not delay your blessing. Esau spent too much time to game for an animal but Jacob swiftly took it with just a goat at their backyard garden. Do not look far for things in order to access your blessing; they might delay you.

WHEN IT'S YOUR TIME, GRAB IT!!!

VALUE Sixteen

HAVING THE SENSE OF VALUE
DIVINE SPEED

Do you not know that those who run in a race all run, but only one receives the prize? Run in such a way that you may win.

1 Corinthians 9:24

Knowing your destiny and purpose in life is not enough. Having insight into the journey ahead of you is also not enough. It should be your prayer that God adds unto you, divine speed in all your endeavours.

You can never become a champion in life, if you do not desire to run. You need to put yourself into action. Work out your destiny and purpose here on earth with maximum speed. Practically, be involved and diligently work out your life's course. Divine speed will get you to the finish line.

During my college days, people could sleep in the library, all in the name of "mining" their books but it was the end of semester results that showed the committed runners. The tape at the finish line is not interested in you sleeping at the library nor your level of information or determination. It is only interested in who breasts it first.

Run the vision of your life. Failure to do so means the vision will run out of your life. Divine speed is the way up and out of stagnation. You can never make a withdrawal at the bank, if you have not made a deposit. Same as there is no output without first making an input, there is no harvest time without first a seed time. So, run to obtain the prize.

DIVINE SPEED: GOD'S OWN ACCELERATION

VALUE Seventeen

HAVING THE SENSE OF VALUE
THE POWER OF IMAGINATION

The LORD said to Abram, after Lot had separated from him, "Now lift up your eyes and look from the place where you are, northward and eastward and westward; for all the land which you see, I will give it to you and your descendants forever.
Genesis 13:14-15

Imagination forms part of life. The bible said emphatically that: "For as a man thinketh in his heart, so is he" – it simply means that you are what you think.

Imagination is the build-up of a mental image of something that is neither perceived as real nor present to the senses. This is a formation to success as the bible text above shows.

You can never be a successful person if you don't think of success. To be successful, first think of success and see it as attainable. God knew of this law and that was why He told Abraham to look as far as his eyes could see. Though Abraham's physical eyes could not see too far, God meant him to gauge with his mind's eye or his imagination. It is interesting to note that, all what Abraham imagined or saw that day, became his portion. Abraham didn't walk the length and breadth of the earth but whatsoever his mind imagined, God gave it to him.

Your imagination is very elastic and how far you pull it, is how much you get. Receive a supernatural ability to imagine your dreams and visions into reality.

> *For as he thinks within himself, so he is. He says to you, "Eat and drink!" But his heart is not with you.*
> *Proverbs 23:7*

IMAGINATION: FUNDAMENTAL TO SUCCESS

VALUE Eighteen

HAVING THE SENSE OF VALUE
THE POWER OF VISION

He who walks blamelessly will be delivered, but he who is crooked will fall all at once.
Proverbs 29:18

Vision is the guide of life. It is the map to follow, if success is to be achieved. Where there is no vision, guide is absent and in the end, life is lived anyhow.

Visions are dreams and foresight to any plans made. The strength of everyone's life lies in the vision he or she carries. To be powerful and influential, you have to carry a vision. Men without vision are of less influence.

Vision is your eyesight, therefore without it, you are blind. The unknown future can be viewed through the lens of vision, though many times, the images are far off from us. As a guide, when we go step by step to approach whatever image we saw, it gradually takes shape and becomes a reality.

You are the master of your vision. What you see, sometimes your followers cannot even see. Vision can be shared but mastery of handling it is the hands of the visionary. When you master your vision, no one can easily switch you off the track. Visions are opened for criticisms. Observers will always be worried because they do not comprehend your vision.

VISION: LIFE'S CONTAINER!

> *"For the vision is yet for the appointed time; It hastens toward the goal and it will not fail. Though it tarries, wait for it; For it will certainly come, it will not delay.*
>
> *Habakkuk 2:3*

Never trade your vision to your critics. Do not succumb to the comments of your oppossers, because of what you perceive to achieve. Not all men will understand and even buy into what you carry.

Everybody has two eyeballs made in different shape and sizes. Your nose is different from mine. Your choices will therefore not be the same as your biological siblings. It is one's dream to build a 2 bedroom apartment one day, whiles another person's dream is to own a Gated community. Understand that everybody carries something different.

The blindman Bartimeus envisioned seeing. Therefore, despite how much the people shouted at him to keep quiet, his dream made him burst out the more because he perceived that all that he needed to get him to gain his eyesight was available. Let no one hinder you in your vision. If people curtail your sense of vision, they have succeeded in rendering you powerless.

It is true that the vision is slated for an appointed time. Though it has the tendency to tarry, do wait for it, for as you hold on it, it shall surely speak. Never drop your vision, lest one day your voice will not be heard.

YOUR VISION IS YOUR VOICE!
Everybody is a leader as per the vision carried. To be successful means you must lead your vision into reality. Never bang your vision on people and think that they will bring your dreams into reality for you.

Entrusting your vision solely into the hands of people does not speak well of your future. Your dreams cannot become realities if you fail to exercise authority. Every driver sits behind the wheels with the focus to get to the final destination. In the same vein, a dream without a focus is not worth living for.

The vision of the four men was to get the leper to where Jesus was. Though the porches and galleries were filled with people, they were not deterred from making their dream a reality. They master-minded their vision and when they needed to re-strategize their cause, they easily made it to the goal. No matter the obstacles, persist to lead your dream into reality because you carry that power.

LEAD OUT YOUR VISION!

VALUE Nineteen

HAVING THE SENSE OF VALUE
PLAYING TO DIVINE ADVANTAGE

In all your ways acknowledge Him, And he will make your paths straight

Proverbs 3:6

One of the greatest channels to our greatness is to play to divine advantage. The preparedness of every individual to make it in life speaks volumes of how life has been marked out seriously by that person.

Many people miss out daily on how to play to divine advantage. God has a plan for everybody and the promises of God are to give us an expected end. A God who knows the end from the beginning cannot bestow into our hands, mandates full of purpose, authority, pathways to emerge victorious and promises of blessings if that was not needed.

To play to divine advantage means you have to know what God has said about you, work at it in obedience and move in line with God's timing. The harlot played to divine advantage by acknowledging she was a sinner and unworthy to come under Jesus' feet. Zacchaeus handed over his treasury just to fall into divine advantage.

He who dwells in prayer is divinely advantaged. Seeking for wisdom and knowledge aligns you to divine advantage. Humility, respect, obedience, faithfulness, selflessness, giving, righteousness and love, strategically bring you into the divine agenda of God.

VALUE Twenty

VIRTUE OF LIFE
DWELLING IN MEEKNESS

> *Remind them to be subject to rulers, to authorities, to be obedient, to be ready for every good deed, to malign no one, to be peaceable, gentle, showing every consideration for all men.*
>
> *Titus 3:1-2*

Living a life full of meekness is very important. In today's world people live with no sense of meekness. Many people have lost it on the essence of life.

Righteousness, humility, patience, gentleness and our ability to stand the test of time, no matter the sufferings and pain we go through, are essential keys to success. Jesus Christ cautioned his disciples and us all to be meek in all our endeavours. A life full of meekness is what the Lord desires.

See to it daily, that you walk and dwell in meekness. Meekness cannot be seen unless it is lived and acted out. Tolerate one another, be calm in your utterances, submit to authorities, give yourself to sound doctrines and teachings, be of sweet and gentle spirit. Above all trust in God.

A true disciple of God walks in meekness. Are you one? You alone know where you fall. Mirror yourself and see where exactly you stand. If you find any error, just re-align yourself. If you are in line, seek to be clothed more and more in meekness. Soon the King of glory comes, coming for a church without spots or wrinkles. We are the church and a church without meekness will not be counted by God.

God's command to us to be meek was never a suggestion therefore you and I have no option than to live in meekness.

DWELLING IN MEEKNESS: GOD'S DESIRE FOR MANKIND

VALUE Twenty One

VIRTUE OF LIFE
LIVING AT PEACE WITH ALL MEN

> *"Peace I leave with you; My peace I give to you; not as the world gives do I give to you. Do not let your heart be troubled, nor let it be fearful.*
>
> *John 14:27*

Peace is an essential commodity in every human society. Wherever there is peace, there also exists harmony, unity and love. We all need peace in every facet of our lives.

Whenever nations war against each other, destruction triumphs over peaceful coexistence. Even the human body needs peace for proper growth. Life's issues mostly fight against our peace.

Jesus Christ has been our perfect example with respect to the peace factor. Even at Jesus' arrest, He fixed the ear of an opponent.

When the disciples forebade people to share the gospel, Jesus killed that joy in them for the sake of peace. of peace.

> *Simon Peter then, having a sword, drew it and struck the high priest's slave, and cut off his right ear; and the slave's name was Malchus. So Jesus said to Peter, "Put the sword into the sheath; the cup which the Father has given Me, shall I not drink it?" So the Roman cohort and the commander and the officers of the Jews, arrested Jesus and bound Him*
> *John 18:10-12*

PEACE BE UNTO YOU today and always!!!

VALUE Twenty Two

VIRTUE OF LIFE
WAITING

Gathering them together, He commanded them not to leave Jerusalem, but to wait for what the Father had promised, "Which," He said, "you heard from Me; for John baptized with water, but you will be baptized with the Holy Spirit not many days from now." So when they had come together, they were asking Him, saying, "Lord, is it at this time You are restoring the kingdom to Israel? He said to them, "It is not for you to know times or epochs which the Father has fixed by His

> *own authority; but you will receive power when the Holy Spirit has come upon you; and you shall be My witnesses both in Jerusalem, and in all Judea and Samaria, and even to the remotest part of the earth."*
>
> *Acts 1:4-8*

Life is a process and we must patiently go through it.

The subject of waiting is very relevant in our daily life. Our aim to be great one day is a promise in itself and therefore we go through life, waiting for that glorious age.

If one is to become a lawyer or an engineer, that person must give him or herself to the process of learning while awaiting that accolade.

In waiting, we are expected not to be idle but to diligently give ourselves to activities that are worthwhile.

In the period of waiting, run with the promise, identify your place of glory, protect your vision, stick to plan and lean on God. Waiting gives us experiences, as well as toughening and preparing us in the broader sense.

The Apostles of Jesus were to wait for the promise in order for them to be solid in their calling.

Do not rush to make it in life. When you give yourself to process, you will reach your destination. It is said that the greatest commission in life is 'to Go ye therefore' but without 'A wait ye' there will not be any meaningful 'Go ye'. The period of waiting prepares us adequately for the future.

Creation is still awaiting the manifestation of the sons of the living God and it will not take a twinkle of an eye for your future to come into being, even though your end is a finished work unto God.

If God is still waiting for you to manifest the end He destined for you, why can't you allow life to take its course and wait for your greatness in the end?

Mary, the mother of Jesus had to wait patiently for the promised Messiah. James, John, Thomas, Peter, Matthew, James the son of Alphaeus, Simon Zelotes, and Judas the brother of James all had to wait for power.

There are too many unprepared people working in the corporate world, lots of unqualified people in politics and many people preaching the gospel without a message.

You are not too big to wait. Go and wait for power which is God's dynamic influence that brings change.

> *Then they returned to Jerusalem from mount called Olivet, which is near Jerusalem, a Sabbath day's journey away. When they had entered the city, they went up to the upper room where they*

were staying; that is Peter and John and James and Andrew, Philip and Thomas, Bartholomew and Matthew, James the son of Alphaeus, and Simon the Zealot, and Judas the son of James. These all with one mind were continually devoting themselves to prayer, along with the women, and Mary the mother of Jesus, and with His brothers.
Acts 1: 12-14

VALUE Twenty Three

VIRTUE OF LIFE
LOYALTY

Do not let kindness and truth leave you; Bind them around your neck, Write them on the tablet of your heart. So you will find favor and good repute in the sight of God and man. Trust in the LORD with all your heart and do not lean on your own understanding. In all your ways acknowledge Him, And He will make your path straight. Do not be wise in your own eyes; Fear the LORD and turn away from evil. It will be healing to your body And refreshment to your bones. Honor the LORD from your wealth and from the first of all your produce; So your barns

will be filled with plenty And your vats will overflow with new wine. My son, do not reject the discipline of the LORD or loathe His reproof, For whom the LORD love He reproves, Even as a father corrects the son in whom he delights. How blessed is the man who finds wisdom and the man who gains understanding.
Proverbs 3: 3-13

Loyalty is commitment and faithfulness to a person or a cause. Those who are loyal to their families, friends, organizations, country and their God, stand by and support them at all times, be it good or bad. They can be counted on, when the going gets tough and they can be trusted to help out when the chips are down.

Life without a sense of loyalty is not worth living. Be loyal at your workplace, in your marriage, in your local church and in your society. Let your faithfulness count in all things. On the font of ministry, let loyalty lead. Be committed in whatever you do.

If things are not moving as expected, do check your sense of loyalty; something may be missing in there. I am yet to witness someone who has been loyal and has gone unrewarded.

Disloyalty brings shame and disgrace but loyalty moves God to fortify us. When you stay faithful in all things, God has no choice than to reward you bountifully.

LOYALTY IS BAIT FOR GREATNESS!

VALUE Twenty Four

VIRTUE OF LIFE
RESPECT

Honor all people, love the brotherhood, fear God, honor the king.

1 Peter 2:17

Respect is honoring the worth and dignity of all people. Those who respect others, treat them with fairness and courtesy. They treat others just as they wish to be treated.

Life demands respect. Whatever you respect, you attract. One of the greatest gifts you can give is to respect yourself and others. Respect is earned, not taken. It is common knowledge that, the more respect you give the more respect you earn. When you respect people, you have sown seeds in their lives; therefore you will reap of its fruits. Do not expect to be respected if you have not sown that seed.

No matter the circumstances in life, never disregard people, even at their worst provocations or attitudes. Respect must be mutual otherwise, you enslave the other party.

Respect those in authority, give reverence to your spouse, and respect the views of your children and others.

When you respect, you fulfill righteousness. Let your level of respect be proper and God will honor you.

VALUE Twenty Five

VIRTUE OF LIFE
OBEDIENCE

"Hear, O Israel! The LORD is our God, the LORD is one! "You shall love the LORD your God with all your soul and with all your might. These words, which I am commanding you today, shall be on your heart. "You shall teach them diligently to your sons and shall talk of them when you sit in your house and when you walk by the way and when you lie down and when you rise up. "You shall bind them as a sign on your hand they shall be as frontals on your forehead. "You shall write them on the doorposts of your house and on your gates".

Deuteronomy 6:4-9

To obey is better than sacrifice. Without obedience, there cannot be any straight or worthy cause in life.

Obedience is compliance to the plan; conformity to the pattern; observance of the rules; adherence to the standards; and submission to another's will.

Obedience is the "bottom line" in Christian life. Basic to every decision we make is the necessity of knowing what scripture says about the issue, what action God wants us to take, what attitude would please God, and what steps are required.

To obey means doing what God says, in the timing and manner He says to do it. We must, then, know what God's instructions are. We cannot comply with something we do not understand. Though many-a-time we do not understand God, we still have to be obedient. It is the Holy Spirit that assists us in relating God's commands to our situation and helps us in determining the wisest course of action.

Whenever you are tempted to disobey God, your faithfulness, devotion and love for Christ are at stake. Ask yourself: 'Is my understanding of Scripture increasing?, Am I able to hold on to God's plan without compromise? How committed am I to obeying Him? Let us be swift to obey the statutes of God and not to compromise on our most holy faith; for delay in obedience is disobedience. When we trust and obey, there is a glory God sheds on our way and out of our obedience, He abides with us always!

VALUE Twenty Six

VIRTUE OF LIFE
PATIENCE

Arise, O LORD; SAVE ME, O my God! For you have smitten all my enemies on the cheek; You have shattered the teeth of the wicked.

Psalm 37:7

Patience is a key virtue in life. A life rushed can be crashed at any time. Life is not like a cafeteria where you pay before you get served but it is like a restaurant where you go through the menu, sit patiently and wait to be served.

The Holy Spirit produces patience in us. In the cycle of life, we should understand that we all cannot be served at the same time. As a matter of fact, your turn of blessing will not be my turn. The materialization of your dream and visions does not mean my time has come too.

Patience therefore is the ability to wait, endure and persevere calmly when faced with any difficulties, without becoming annoyed or upset. When you patiently go through life's processes, your turn will surely come.

No great man or woman never cooked their life suddenly, but became great with time. You may be praying for the fruit of the womb; just wait a little while. It looks as if the vision has delayed, but bear in mind that it is set for an appointed time, therefore though it tarries, wait for it.

PATIENCE IS THE EYE OF WISDOM!

Patience solidifies our foundations in life. The life built on patience is excellent.

It is only patience that opens the door of greatness. Prayer alone cannot redeem our days which are evil. A daily sense of patience is very necessary in our everyday lives.

I have come to believe that most competitions, monopolies and fights for seeking vainglory at the workplace, church, home and society is due to lack of patience.

Patience is being tolerant enough, looking out for the right and set time for your manifestation. Patience must incite us to build a strong future. Patience affects our reasoning patterns, builds a sense of evaluation in us, throws us into our focus in life, makes us considerate and helps us to settle on which path to take.

PATIENCE: THE LIFE BUILDER!

James, a bond-servant of God and of the Lord Jesus Christ, to the twelve tribes who are dispersed abroad: Greetings. Consider it all joy, my brethren, when you encounter various trials, knowing that the testing of you faith produces endurance. And let endurance have its perfect results, so that you may be perfect and complete, lacking in nothing. But if any of you lacks wisdom, let him ask of God, who gives to all generously and without reproach, and it will be given to him. James 1:1-5

It is said that patience yields victory. This means that in patience, there is success.

Many people have missed a lot of opportunities due to lack of patience. Life is such that without a close look at things, you will continue to make mistakes and miss out on a lot.

Life's brake is patience. Patience slows us down whenever we seem to be rushing in life and even in our moves to outrun God. Patience tests our level of hope, faith and perseverance and this leads us to steadfastness. The full effect of steadfastness makes us lack nothing. God is not slow to save you from your troubles as you may think; He only deals with us in patience. When you bear with God, He also bears with you.

PATIENCE: LIFE'S VITAMINS

> *I thank Christ Jesus our Lord, who has strengthened me, because He considered me faithful, putting me into service, even though I was formerly a blasphemer and a persecutor and a violent aggressor. Yet I was shown mercy because I acted ignorantly in unbelief; and the grace of our Lord was more than abundant, with the faith and love which are found in Christ Jesus. It is a trustworthy statement, deserving full acceptance, that Christ Jesus came into the world to save sinners, among whom I am foremost of all. Yet for this reason I found mercy, so that in me as the foremost, Jesus Christ might demonstrate His perfect patience as an example for those who would believe In Him for eternal life. Now to the King eternal, immortal, invisible, the only God, be honor and glory forever and ever. Amen.*
> *1 Timothy 1:12-17*

We are to bear one another in patience. A fruitful and lasting relationship cannot be achieved if the habit of patience is not cultivated.

If indeed love is patient, then it will only take enough patience to keep a barren wife, a nagging husband, a snobbish boss, a naive friend, difficult and troublesome family.

Patience is a virtue. It is not easy to bear the load of someone who gets on your nerves but patience makes that burden lighter. Patience is being tolerant and accommodative enough.

God still accommodates us in our numerous weaknesses, troubles and struggles. He bears with us in patience. Jesus had time to attend to the issues of people therefore we must also give ourselves room to carry each other's load.

Thank you for bearing with me even in this Value Series. It takes a lot of patience for you to have come this far with me. I am fully persuaded that, patience you lack not.

> *So, as those who have been chosen of God, holy and beloved, put on a heart of compassion, kindness, humility, gentleness and patience; bearing with one another, and forgiving each other, whoever has a complaint against anyone; just as the Lord forgave you, so also should you.*
> *Colossians 3:12-13*

PATIENCE: THE CONNECTING FORCE!

VALUE Twenty Seven

VIRTUE OF LIFE
CONTENTMENT IS GREAT GAIN

> *"The sheep of a laborer is sweet, whether they eat little or much, but as for the rich, their abundance permits them no sleep. I have seen a grievous evil under the sun: wealth hoarded to the harm of its owners, or wealth lost through some misfortune, so that when they have children there is nothing left for them to inherit."*
>
> Ecclesiastes 5:12

Always be content with what you have. It is a blessing to appreciate whatever you have achieved so far and glory in it Most importantly, learn to acknowledge the God who has brought you this far. Desire to be content with what you have. Never covet what belongs to a brother and do not strive or contend with a neighbour over that which is clearly not yours.

Your state of contentment will prove your mental or emotional state of satisfaction. The Apostle Paul admonishes us to be content daily with what we have to eat, drink and put on - for that alone is enough.

In today's world, lots of people are gathering wealth, contending with people over lands; some taking over people's wives and husbands; others coveting what belongs to a neighbour; and enmity all over due to lack of contentment. All these lead to vexation of spirit. What people forget is that in the end, all is vanity.

It is a great gain when you are content with what you have because it saves you from lots of tension, unnecessary competition, rage, malice and above all your peace becomes absolute.

BE CONTENT ENOUGH AND HUMBLY ASK GOD FOR MORE!!!

VALUE Twenty Eight

VIRTUE OF LIFE
COMMITMENT

"Now, Israel, what does the LORD your God require from you, but to fear the LORD your God, to walk in all His ways and love Him, and to serve the LORD your God with all your heart and with all your soul, and to keep the LORD'S commandments and His statutes which I am commanding you today for your good?
Deuteronomy 10:12-13

Commitment is giving your time and energy to something valuable out of your own free will. It is a level of loyalty, promise, dedication or pledging allegiance to something.

A successful life runs on commitment. Whatever you do not commit to does not deserve your attention, time, energy and money. Commitment is a seed that germinates its own fruits. If you sow a seed of trustworthiness and honesty in your life, it will attract many people to confide in you.

When the disciples of Jesus committed to him, He appointed them unto a Kingdom. Commitment therefore qualifies you for appointment. Failure to commit to the choices you have made in life means you are not expecting any achievements. Naturally, commitment is a trigger for achievement.

A consistent investment of energy, time and resources into your choices, produces great outcomes. There is no success without hardwork. To be successful, you must work diligently at your choices, giving them all the inputs they require.

> *And they approached the village where they were going, and He acted as though He were going farther. But they argued Him saying. "Stay with us, for it is getting towards evening, and the day is nearly over." So He went in to stay with them.*

When He had reclined at the table with them, He took the bread and blessed it, and breaking it, He began giving it to them.

Luke 22:28-30

COMMITMENT: THE ANCHOR OF ACHIEVEMENTS!

VALUE Twenty Nine

VIRTUE OF LIFE
THE SPIRIT OF SACRIFICE

And do not neglect doing good and sharing, for with such sacrifices God is pleased.
Hebrews 13:16

It is a good thing to live with a spirit of sacrifice. Not everybody has this spirit. It is one thing having the gift of sacrifice and another carrying the spirit of sacrifice.

The spirit of sacrifice always gives the notch to sacrifice. Its operation is very dominating and possessing. The gift can consume but the spirit offers total dominion. People have the gift to sacrifice; therefore they go to their wits end to sacrifice. However, at the brink of any disappointments or hitches, there comes a sense of withdrawal. Living with a spirit of sacrifice means your level of sacrifice will know no boundaries, no matter the inconveniences you face.

The gift can be used or not, but the spirit possesses and dominates till the end. Those who live in the spirit of sacrifice do not dwell on hearsays in order to do good or not. The spirit of sacrifice leads beyond inconsistencies. It should be your desire to live with the spirit of sacrifice than to merely dwell on the gift of sacrifice.

Anger, bitterness, malice, strife and contentions corrupt the gift of sacrifice. The good news is that in the realm of the spirit of sacrifice, these vices do not triumph. In today's world, a brother cannot genuinely sacrifice for a brother; a daughter for a mother, a friend for a friend, etc., all because the gift of sacrifice fails. There must be a paradigm shift right from the gift of sacrifice into the spirit of sacrifice.

Many people do sacrifice for others because they expect something in return. The gift of sacrifice has thrown a lot of people into unnecessary expectations. As they give out their time, money and resources to people, they are expectant of good rewards in return.

Living with the gift of sacrifice makes people enter into certain negotiations that sometimes destroy the beauty of sacrifice. A man sacrificed to get a job for a young lady and as the job was secured, this man asked that the lady to show appreciation to him in kind. The lady, from the depths of her heart, bought a gift for the man as a sign of gratitude, yet the man showed no contentment because he expected something more.

In the realm of the gift of sacrifice, these things prevail a lot. Everybody looks out to be rewarded for every sacrifice made. How many times have you given out money to people at your own inconvenience, only to receive no appreciation? How did you feel? You felt bad and disappointed, I guess. Human as we are, we demand praise for our sacrifices.

We cannot continue to live without sacrificing at length. Let us learn to labour for one another without any expectation of kindness in return. The fact that you are good doesn't mean people will always do you good. Sometimes, your sacrifice will cost you but do not cease sacrificing.

The spirit of sacrifice is a realm of total devotion. Jesus Christ got it right and because of that, you cannot produce any negative results.

SPIRIT OF SACRIFICE: A REALM OF TOTAL DEVOTION

> *Do not merely look out for your own personal interests, but also for the interests of others.*
> *Philippians 2:4*

VALUE Thirty

VIRTUE OF LIFE
PUT ON YOUR CONFIDENCE

For I am confident of this very thing, that He who began a good work in you will perfect it until the day of the Christ Jesus
                        Philippians 1:6

One of the greatest elements to face life and its battles with is to be clothed in Confidence. We should learn to be confident in each and every step we take.

Many lives which were full of plans, dreams and visions ended up being crashed, all because carriers of these virtues failed to be confident enough to dispense what they carried. Failure to be confident in your own self, beliefs and visions is disruption in disguise.

Shadrach, Meshach and Abednego trusted what they had believed. They were confident in professing God alone as their Lord and King. It is worth noting that, whatever you believe or trust in and are fully sold out into has the potency to save your life.

Peter initially built confidence to walk on the water to meet Jesus but in the midst of the storm, he began to sink because he was not totally sold out for that cause.

You cannot live here on earth with a shallow level of confidence. Jesus was confident to face his life and ministry, no matter the obstructions laid to derail him. Build your confidence to its maximum capacity to face life.

> *Such confidence we have through Christ toward God*
> *2 Corinthians 3:4*

CONFIDENCE: A SPICE TO LIFE'S SUCCESS

VALUE Thirty One

VIRTUE OF LIFE
DIG AGAIN

"They told him, "Jesus of Nazareth is passing by." He called out, "Jesus, Son of David, have mercy on me!" Those who led the way rebuked him and told him to be quiet, but he shouted all the more, "Son of David, have mercy on me!"

Luke 18:37-39

Never look at your present condition and throw in the towel. Life is never a one-way street. A great level of tenacity makes life worth living.

There is always the need to keep on keeping on, no matter what life presents. Keep on digging until you find water. That job may not be rewarding enough but do not think about quitting. There may be no joy or happiness in that marriage and home but do not consider divorce as an option. You keep trailing that academic paper; however, I encourage you to try again.

While the blindman was asked to keep quiet, his condition made him shout more for a breakthrough. You may be suppressed but keep your hopes and focus alive. Business seems to be failing; just hold up and out. Do not tender in your resignation in that company yet. Rather, reconsider and dig again. In your relationship with others, do not let issues bring separation but dig again for the sake of unity. It will certainly work out as you persevere!

Jesus told Peter to recast his net and as because he did, they had more than enough to feed on. Do not give up or lose your focus. Be determined to dig again.

Epilogue

I believe you have been blessed by this book. Having gone through these values and virtues, you must have noted the great price involved in the quest of man to succeed. To every successful living, there is a price to pay. Value is essentially a function of cost. Nothing of value is for free. Now, there is no time to waste: rise up and give the champion in you a chance of expression.

Rising to the top is a worthy goal so you must be determined to strive to get there. Although the top is open and uncluttered, it takes a strong set of values and virtues to get and stay there.

My utmost desire for writing this book is to recondition your mind, especially, on what you are made up of, to uphold the rule of engagements of life through values and virtues and for you to accept full responsibility of the successful dreams that you have.

Be full of values and virtues, make the right choices, and in the end let me see you at the top!

www.ingramcontent.com/pod-product-compliance
Lightning Source LLC
Chambersburg PA
CBHW070517090426
42735CB00012B/2817